I0805276

# What Would You Do If . . .

*A simple strategy for preparing kids to think and act responsibly*

*Targeted for parents of children ages two to eight*

# What Would You Do If . . .

*A simple strategy for preparing kids to think and act responsibly*

*Targeted for parents of children ages two to eight*

by
Shalmarie Bunker
and Kim Osborne

BONNEVILLE BOOKS ™
Springville, Utah

Copyright © 2002 Shalmarie Bunker and Kim Osborne

All Rights Reserved.

No part of this book may be reproduced in any form whatsoever, whether by graphic, visual, electronic, film, microfilm, tape recording, or any other means, without prior written permission of the author, except in the case of brief passages embodied in critical reviews and articles.

ISBN: 1-55517-588-0
v.1

Published by Bonneville Books
Imprint of Cedar Fort, Inc.
925 N. Main Springville, Utah, 84663
www.cedarfort.com

Distributed by Cedar Fort, Inc.

Typeset by Marny K. Parkin
Cover design by Adam Ford
Cover design © 2001 by Lyle Mortimer

Printed in the United States of America
10 9 8 7 6 5 4 3 2 1

Printed on acid-free paper

Library of Congress Cataloging-in-Publication Data

Bunker, Shalmarie.

What would you do if-- : a simple strategy for preparing kids to think and act responsibly / Shalmarie Bunker and Kim Osborne.

p. cm.

ISBN 1-55517-588-0 (pbk. : alk. paper)

1. Child rearing. 2. Parent and child. 3. Interpersonal communication. I. Osborne, Kim. II. Title.

HQ769 .B778 2002

649'.1--dc21

2001006587

*To our children:*

You are our passion, motivation,
and inspiration.
You have made us become
the best of whom we are.
We give you our love
and our hope.
In return you give us our joy.
It is our hope that we
teach you some small portion
of all that you have taught us.

# Acknowledgments

With gratitude we thank our husbands for their never-ending support, enthusiasm and encouragement. It may not mean retirement, but it is a start. To Marie (a.k.a. Mom), our first-rate research assistant, baby-sitter, cheerleader, and example, we give our thanks, which seems inadequate for all the assistance you have given us. To our parents we say thanks for expecting the best from us. In addition, we give our thanks to all our friends and family, some who may have lent us their children and all who have given their support.

We would also like to acknowledge one another. It is a rare thing to find a friend with whom we can each work so well. Each of our strengths balance the other's weaknesses. Who could have guessed that a simple discussion by the kiddie pool could have sparked us on this journey? Who knows what the future has in store.

# Contents

# Introduction

## *The how and why of What Would You Do If . . .*

"What would you do if you are playing outside and someone you didn't know tells you he lost his puppy and wants your help to find it?"

"I would go and help him, Mama," said my four-year-old daughter Cassidy—without blinking an eye. My stomach turned, tears rolled down my cheeks and I was certain I had failed parenting.

Now take a moment, gather your children around you and ask them the same question. Don't be alarmed if you receive an answer you didn't expect.

As parents, we make assumptions as to what we think we have taught our children and what we think they know. Yet, are we as certain as we think we are? When I asked Cassidy this question did I have an assumption as to what her answer would be? Of course I did. Had we had the "stranger" talk? Yes. Had she learned all that I had hoped—emphatically *no.*

So, the passion behind *What Would You Do If* . . . was born. We set out to develop a simple, practical tool that will assist parents and teachers in educating children in the process of decision-making. It is imperative to prepare our children to adequately face any situation in which they may find themselves.

A great way to begin is by having

your child be an *active participant* in decision making rather than a passive listener. Experts agree that children who are provided with decision-making opportunities while they are young are more likely to be responsible decision makers in the future. So, rather than attempting to engage your child in a *talk* where you talk and they stare out the window, try allowing them to take part in the conversation. For example, you are in the car driving your son to his friend's house:

Parent: "Jason, what would you do if you are at Jacob's house and he wants to show you his dad's gun?"

He may answer, "Cool!" or very possibly, "I don't know." Or even, "He already did."

The truth is, you don't know what he will say and more importantly what he will *do* if you don't ask. He may not know what *to do* if he has never discussed it with you. However, before you begin, ask yourself, what do *I want* his answer to be and why? And then discuss it *with* him. Take time to discuss the consequences of various answers and listen to what ideas your child has. By providing your children with actual scenarios, they are given concrete examples of how to utilize their learning. In addition they are supplied with an atmosphere that will engage them in the learning process.

This book is divided into five chapters. Each chapter focuses on a different area of life where your child will be called upon to make decisions. Make these situations as personal to your children as possible by using some actual names and places they will relate to. "What If

Tips" are included in each chapter. These tips provide you with ways to create meaningful and useful dialogue with your kids. In addition, they include examples of how these questions played out with our own children. Anecdotes from children we have interviewed are also included throughout the book. These are intended to provide you with the type of actual, honest answers that children may give you. They are in no way intended to provide you with "correct" responses that you should hope for from your children.

One unique element in this book is that it empowers you, as a parent; to teach your children based on your belief system not ours. However, if at any time you feel that you are unsure about the correct solution to teach your child, there are countless resources available to you.

For example, your pediatrician, schoolteachers or counselors, local police and fire departments as well as your local library and Internet are all resources that are available to assist you.

In conclusion, make sure to repeat and repeat and repeat! In other words, use each of these questions often. Try a little variation. By slightly changing certain elements (person, place, etc.) you will be able to evaluate your child's understanding of the concepts you are trying to teach. It is only through constant and consistent teaching that your child will begin to develop the decision-making skills that you desire and they will be better prepared to face whatever situations they may encounter.

A child who feels confident in his

ability to make responsible decisions and has been reassured that his sense of judgment is strong will trust his instincts, even in difficult situations. Will they always get it right? Again, I say emphatically *no!* But, they are kids, *your kids*, and as their parent you want to do everything in your power to give them the tools they will need to be safe and successful.

## Chapter 1

# Out of Sight, But Not Out of Mind

### *What would you do if you were at a friend's house and . . .*

This chapter introduces children to situations they may encounter at a friend or relative's house. Situations involve children being away from their parents and may possibly involve an adult other than the parent. These questions allow you to begin discussing the boundaries of respect and authority. These questions also provide you with an opportunity to evaluate the effects of peer pressure on your child.

**Mom:** "Madie, what would you do if you are at 'Ashley's' house and her dad tries to touch your private places?"

**Madie:** "I'd say, 'Don't touch me there.'"

**Mom:** "What if he says, 'It's okay, honey.'"

**Madie:** "I would yell, 'Don't touch me there!'"

**Mom:** "What if he says, 'Shhh! Be quiet, Madie, it's okay.'"

**Madie:** "No, it's not! No, it's not!"

**Mom:** "What if he grabs you and is so strong you cannot get away?"

**Madie:** "Let go of me!"

**Mom:** "What if he was just too strong and he did touch you and then let you go?"

**Madie:** "I'd run and go tell her mom that he touched me and then I'd call you and come home."

**Mom:** "What would you tell Mom when you got home?"

**Madie:** "That he wouldn't let me go and he touched my private places and he wouldn't stop when I said don't touch me!"

*Madie, age five*

***Three quarters of the violent victimizations of children took place in either the victim's home or the offender's home. Approximately one-half of the victimizers had a relationship with the victim as a friend, acquaintance or relative other than offspring.***

***— Bureau of Justice***

**"What If" Tip:**
***Getting Beyond What You Want to Hear***

Many times, especially when beginning to practice problem-solving skills, children may be inclined to provide you with the answer that they assume you want to hear. For example, Madie's first response was "Don't touch me." However, in order to teach your child to think through various possible solutions and consequences, you must find a way to get beyond their initial answer. One way to do that is to continue with the scenario by asking more questions, probing deeper and giving realistic examples of how events may take place.

If you feel this is too overwhelming for your child, simply discuss other solutions or give many different versions of the same situation until they are willing to discuss it further.

***What would you do if you were at a friend's house and . . .***

Your friend wants to play in the trunk of a car

Your friend wants to play inside of a car

Your friend wants to play "hair cut" with real scissors

Your friend wants to play in a stream (river, lake, swimming pool, fountain, etc.)

***Drowning claims the life of four thousand people each year. Children ages zero to four have the highest death rate due to drowning.***

***—National Safety Council***

**Dad:** "What would you do if you are at Kenna's house and she wants to play in the trunk of her mom's car?"

**Madison:** "I would never get in there; it is too dark and scary!"

*Madison, age seven*

***What would you do if you were at a friend's house and . . .***

Your friend wants to play with matches

Your friend wants to play with fireworks

Your friend shows you a gun

Your friend wants to ride bikes but you don't have your helmet

***The Bicycle Helmet Safety Institute states that Bicycle Helmets can prevent 88 percent of cyclists' brain injuries. Head injuries cause about 75 percent of all bicycling fatalities.***

***—National Safety Council***

**Mom:** "Jodi, what would you do if you are at a friend's house and your friend wants to show you a gun?"

**Jodi:** "I'd run as fast as I could and get a Mommy or Daddy!"

*Jodi, age five*

***It is estimated that one-half of all American households have fire-arms. Most children kill themselves or other children unintentionally while they are playing with a gun found in their home or the home of a friend.***

***— National Safety Council***

***What would you do if you were at a friend's house and . . .***

You are hungry/thirsty

Your friend gives you food that you are not allowed to eat

Your friend gives you food you do not like

You spill your drink/food

***What would you do if you were at a friend's house and . . .***

You get sick

You wet your pants

Your friend gets sick

You get hurt

***What would you do if you were at a friend's house and . . .***

Your friend starts hitting you

Your friend starts calling you names

You want to go home and your friend won't let you

It is time to go home and you don't want to

***What would you do if you were at a friend's house and . . .***

Your friend wants to watch a movie that scares you

Your friend turns on a show you are not allowed to watch

You want a toy that your friend is playing with

You break your friend's toy

**Mom:** "What would you do if you are at Katie's house and she turns on a movie you are not allowed to watch?"

**Alexander:** "I would say, 'I can't watch this.'"

*Alexander, age two*

***What would you do if you were at a friend's house and . . .***

Your friend shows you pictures that make you uncomfortable

You and your friend find pictures on the computer that make you uncomfortable

Your friend's mom wants to take you somewhere but you don't have your car seat/seat belt

You find out your friend's parents are not home

**Dad:** "Joseph, what would you do if you are playing at Matt's house and his mom wants to take you somewhere but you don't have your car seat?"

**Joseph:** "I would call you and tell you to bring it over."

*Joseph, age three*

***What would you do if you were at a friend's house and . . .***

The smoke alarm goes off

Your friend wants to take your panties/underwear off to play doctor

Your friend's mom/dad/sibling touches your private places

You are walking home and you think you are being followed

**Shalmarie's "What If" Payoff**

I was busily cleaning up the family room when I heard several knocks at the door. I answered it to find my daughter breathless and flushed. I asked her what was wrong. She said she had seen a gun at her friend's house where she had been playing. She explained that she had done as I had taught her and ran straight home.

Just then the phone rang. It was my neighbor wondering why my daughter had ran from her home so frantically. I explained to her what my daughter had seen and expressed my concern. She said she was equally concerned because they do not own a gun. At that same moment, her son walked upstairs carrying the "weapon" a rather realistic looking *squirt* gun.

Although *this* situation did not save my daughter's life, the fact that she put her knowledge and skills to good use made me realize that the "What Would You Do If" conversations were working.

# Chapter 2
# **School Daze**

*What would you do if you were at school and . . .*

This chapter contains situations that your children may encounter as they enter the school setting. These questions address situations where unfamiliar elements may exist. Events include various social interactions that may be new to children. Your discussions may focus on empathy and how we choose to treat others.

**Dad:** "Nicole what would you do if you are at preschool and a bully picks on your friend?"

**Nicole:** "I would say, 'Hey, be nice to her!' Then we would walk away."

Moments later:

**Nicole:** "Dad, there *is* a bully at my school."

**Dad:** "Why is he a bully?"

**Nicole:** "He is always mean to the kids in my class."

**Dad:** "Is he mean to you?"

**Nicole:** "Sometimes."

*Nicole, age four*

From here we were able to discuss what had been happening at school and what steps could be taken to assist her with this problem.

**"What If" Tip:**
***Sharing Surprise***

Many times you may have opened the proverbial "can of worms" without even knowing it. Often times, children may not know exactly how to express or explain what may be happening to them, yet once they are presented with a familiar situation, they recognize it and feel comfortable sharing their experience. Although the parent in this scenario is close with his daughter, until this conversation, her father was unaware of the bully at school. When this type of "sharing" happens don't be alarmed or act surprised. It is important to maintain the safe, comfortable setting that allowed your child to "share" in the first place. If you suspect something may be going on with your child, phrase a question to her about it. If she expounds on it, great—if not, don't push it. Many times your pushing will only make her more reticent to disclose any information to you. Bring this situation up at a later date when you feel she may be more willing to share.

***What would you do if you were at school and . . .***

A bully picks on you

A bully picks on your friend or sibling

Your friend starts being unkind to you

Some of your classmates starts using “bad” words

Someone on the bus takes your lunch

You leave your backpack on the bus

The bus driver forgets to drop you off

You get off at the wrong bus stop

***What would you do if you were at school and . . .***

You miss the bus to school/on the way home from school

Your friend at the bus stop dares you to run in front of the bus

You get sick at school

You wet your pants at school

***School bus related crashes killed 128 and injured nineteen thousand in 1997. Of the pedestrians killed in school bus related crashes, approximately 76 percent were struck by the school bus.***

***—The National Highway Traffic Safety Administration***

***What would you do if you were at school and . . .***

You forget your homework

You forget your lunch

You forget your lunch money

You forget your show and tell

**Teacher:** "What would you do if you forget to bring your show and tell to school?"

**Isabel:** "I take my backpack to school everyday, I can show my backpack and tell them all about it."

*Isabel, age six*

***What would you do if you were at school and . . .***

You can't find your coat for recess/to go home

You notice a stranger watching you while you are playing outside

Your teacher calls you by the wrong name

Your teacher accuses you of something you didn't do (cheating, stealing, hitting, etc.)

***What would you do if you were at school and . . .***

Your teacher suddenly looks sick and falls to the floor

You walk into your classroom and your regular teacher is not there

The power goes off

Smoke alarm goes off

***What would you do if you were at school and . . .***

Someone you do not know tells you that he/she is there to pick you up

While walking home you notice someone following you

The friends you usually walk home with have left you

While waiting for the bus a woman in her car stops and asks you to come talk to her

***The National Safety Council suggests teaching kids to yell or run to a friend's house or near-by store if they feel in danger.***

***What would you do if you were at school and . . .***

You see a child in your class with no one to play with

Someone pushes you and your teacher is busy

Your very best friend doesn't show up at school

You see one of your classmates is crying

**Mom:** "What would you do if you see a child in your class crying?"

**Kay:** "I would go be her friend so she wouldn't cry any more."

*Kay, age five*

***What would you do if you were at school and . . .***

One of the older kids shows you his/her private parts and wants you to show him/her yours

You are offered a piece of candy and after eating it you begin to feel very strange

A teacher/other student tries to touch you in your private places

You find a cigarette on the playground

Someone new shows up in your class

There is a child in your class who cannot hear and uses her/his hands to talk

There is a child in your class who cannot see and uses a cane and/or a special dog

Someone in your class speaks differently than you do

***What would you do if you were at school and . . .***

You can't see what your teacher is writing on the chalkboard

You can't hear what your teacher is saying

You need to use the bathroom really bad

You feel as though you may get sick

## Shalmarie's "What If" Payoff

Various events will arise in the lives of you and your children. As these come up you will see areas to invent your own *What Would You Do If* scenarios. For example, I recently had my daughter fitted for glasses. Having worn glasses my entire life, I tried to be sensitive to some of the situations that she may face. On the first day that she was planning to wear them to school I had the following encounter:

"Cassidy, what will you do if your friends want to try on your glasses at school today?"

She paused for a moment.

"I don't know, Mom. I want to share and be nice but I know they cost a lot of money and I don't want them to get broken. What do you think I should do?"

"Well, I think it is great that you want to share. But you are right they cost a lot of money and can get broken easily. How about if you said to your friends, 'I am glad that you like my new glasses, but my Mom told me that I need to keep them on so that they don't get broken.'"

"Okay, Mom, that sounds good."

A few hours later when I picked her up from school she jumped in the car with a big smile!

"Mom, guess what?"

"What, honey?"

"The kids at school did just like you said they would, they all asked if they could try on my glasses. I knew just what to say, Mom. You were right!"

I smiled, I beamed, my heart swelled. She just uttered the words *you were right!* But even more than that she had confidence in herself and she gained confidence in my ability to teach her. She was faced with a situation and she was prepared.

# Chapter 3
# **Emergency Exits**

## *What would you do in an emergency if . . .*

The aim of this chapter is to provide you with opportunities to discuss what may be frightening or difficult subjects. These questions contain crucial situations that can provide life saving information. By utilizing these questions often, changing slight elements (place, person, etc.) you can help to ensure that your child has a more complete understanding of the whole concept that you are trying to teach. In addition, phrase these questions as if a parent or other adult were available and if the child were alone. Families can use these questions as a lead-in for making clear plans for specific emergency situations.

**Mom:** "Lily, what would you do if you wake up and smell smoke?"

**Lily:** "I would stop, drop, and roll."

*Lily, age four*

**"What If" Tip:**
***Evaluate Understanding***

Your child's answer may often provide a window into their understanding and processing of information. In the above situation, Lily could remember that "stop, drop, and roll" had something to do with fire safety, yet she could not properly utilize the information in the appropriate moment. This type of opportunity will allow you to assess your child's understanding of emergency plans and situations and make sure their understanding is complete.

***What would you do in an emergency if . . .***

The smoke alarm at home goes off

You open your bedroom door and there is fire in the hallway

You wake up and smell smoke

Someone is cooking in the kitchen and you see flames

**Dad**: "What would you do if you wake up and smell smoke?"

**Bronson:** "Run to the family safe spot, then get a neighbor to call 911."

*Bronson, age six*

***What would you do in an emergency if . . .***

Your house is on fire, you get out safely but you realize your sibling/parent/pet is inside

Your friend/sibling/parent/animal catches on fire

You were on fire

You see your friend/sibling playing with matches

***Fires and burns are the third leading cause of unintentional injury death at home.***

***—National Safety Council***

***What would you do in an emergency if . . .***

You get burned

Your mom/dad/baby-sitter is cooking and they get burned

You see your sibling trying to touch the hot stove

Your little brother/sister is in the tub and is trying to turn on the hot water

***What would you do in an emergency if . . .***

You are playing and you get cut

Your mom/dad/sibling/baby-sitter is bleeding and hurt

You can't wake up your mom/dad/sibling/baby-sitter

You are locked out of the house

You/your friend/sibling get locked in the car and can't get out

You are riding in the car and suddenly the driver (mom/dad) slumps over and can't drive

Your friend/sibling takes the lid off the bathroom cleaner

You see your sibling eating pills out of the medicine bottle

***Poisonings from solids and liquids such as drugs, medicines, poisonous house plants, and commonly recognized poisons caused sixty-three hundred deaths in the home in 1998 alone.***

***—National Safety Council***

**Mom:** "What would you do if you are locked in the car and can't get out?"

**Jaxon:** "I'd unlock the door."

**Mom:** "What if it won't open?"

**Jaxon:** "I'd roll down the window."

**Mom:** "What if it is locked?"

**Jaxon:** "Then I'd honk the horn!"

*Jaxon, age eight*

***What would you do in an emergency if . . .***

You see your friend/sibling fall in the swimming pool, canal or river

You and your friend go for a walk, you get lost and can't find your way home

You are playing and you feel the ground start to shake

You hear a loud siren go off (tornado warning, etc.)

**Dad:** "What would you do if you see your friend fall in the swimming pool?"

**Jacob:** "I would jump in and save him."

*Jacob, age four*

***Drowning is the second leading cause of injury related death in children.***

***— Centers for Disease Control***

***What would you do in an emergency if . . .***

You are eating treats and suddenly you can't breathe

You see your friend's/sibling's/parent's face turn blue

You see a neighbor working in the yard and suddenly he fell down and can't get up

You see a child who appears lost

## Kim's "What If" Payoff

Recently, I was outside working in the garden. The kids were playing in the yard and soon wandered into the garage. Knowing the dangers that exist there I quickly followed them. I stood behind the door and listened, curious to see if our *What Would You Do If* practicing would pay off. I heard the car door open and close. My two-year-old had climbed inside. Immediately I heard my five-year-old scream, "Get out, Alex! We are never supposed to play in the car!" She tried to open the door but it was locked. She then ran frantically out of the garage yelling for me to get him out. Because we had already discussed this situation, she was prepared. She took the steps we had discussed and handled the situation perfectly and safely! What a payoff in "What Would You Do If" communication.

Chapter 4

# Let's Go Fly a Kite

*What would you do if you were at the park and . . .*

This chapter addresses very specific situations your child may encounter in a park or playground setting where a parent or teacher may or may not be present.

**Dad:** "What would you do if you are at the park and someone you don't know asks you to help him find his kitty?"

**Kylee:** "I would go and help him find the kitty."

*Kylee, age five*

**"What If" Tip:**
***Naive Nonsense***

None of us are thrilled about the prospects of destroying our child's innocence—yet not providing our children with tools to prepare themselves in potentially difficult or dangerous situations is ignorant and irresponsible at best. We are not doing our children any favors by allowing them to remain naive about potential dangers that exist. By frankly and firmly discussing realistic possibilities that may occur, our children will be better prepared to cope with and hopefully escape these situations.

***What would you do if you were at the park and . . .***

You are swinging and another child is waiting for the swing

You are waiting and another child is swinging

Someone takes your sand toys/ball, etc.

Someone takes your turn on the slide/swings

***What would you do if you were at the park and . . .***

You find a **ball** that is not yours—but you want to play with it

Your ball rolls into the street

Someone takes your turn on the slide/swings

You are playing a game and see a child who is by himself, watching you play

**Mom:** "What would you do if you're playing outside and your ball rolls into the street?"

**Alex:** "I would go tell Mom to get it because cars would squish me!"

*Alex, age two*

***What would you do if you were at the park and . . .***

You see a dog that you don't know coming towards you

A dog bites you

You see someone else get bit by a dog

You see two dogs get into a fight and they start to hurt each other

***What would you do if you were at the park and . . .***

You are eating snacks and your friends don't have any

Someone you don't know offers you a treat

An older kid offers you a drink but it smells/tastes funny

Someone you don't know asks you to help him find his lost puppy/kitty/child, etc.

**Mom:** "What would you do if you are at the park and you see a dog you didn't know coming toward you?"

**Allie:** "I would pet it and tickle it all over."

*Allie, age three*

***What would you do if you were at the park and . . .***

Someone wants to take you for a ride in their car

Someone wants to take you for a ride on his motorcycle

Someone you don't know wants to borrow your bike/scooter

A neighbor wants you to come with them to look at some pictures

***What would you do if you were at the park and . . .***

A grown-up you don't know asks you your name and where you live

You see some older kids smoking and they want you to try it

You find a cigarette

You fall and get hurt

You see someone else fall and get hurt

***Each year approximately two hundred eighty thousand children will be treated in hospital emergency rooms for injuries involving playground equipment and surfacing. Sixty-two percent of these injuries are the result of falls.***

***—National Safety Council***

***What would you do if you were at the park and . . .***

Other kids are playing a game and you want to play

Someone shows you his or her private parts

The kids you are playing with start using "bad words"

**Dad:** "Elle, what would you do if you are playing at the park and the kids you are with start saying bad words?"

**Elle:** "I would say, 'Stop saying that—it is not nice.' If they didn't stop I would go find someone else to play with."

*Elle, age six*

**Shalmarie's "What If" Payoff**

My son and his friend were playing at a park across the street. As I stood on the porch to check on them, I saw a stray dog wandering through the park. My son's friend began running *toward* the dog. My son began yelling at his playmate to leave the dog alone and follow him home. His friend refused, but my son walked quickly home. I was pleased that even in the face of peer pressure my son followed the plan that I had discussed with him. I had given him a clear plan and he used it when the situation arose.

# Chapter 5
# **Out and About**

## *What would you do if . . .*

This chapter contains a variety of situations children may come across when dealing with the public or in various public settings.

**Mom:** "What would you do if you get lost in the grocery store?"

**Cassandra:** "I would pray that I could find you."

**Mom:** "What else can you do?"

**Cassandra:** "I could find a cash register and tell the person there that I am lost."

*Cassandra, age five*

**"What If" Tip:**
***Practice Time***

A great way to utilize the questions in this section is through role-play. For example, as you drive to the grocery store ask your children, "What would you do if you get lost in the store?" Listen to their answers and discuss what you feel is the best possible solution. Let's assume that your solution was to have them find a check out clerk. As your enter the store have your children point out where the check out counters are and repeat to you what information they would tell them (name, parents name, etc.). Being able to visualize their plan in action their confidence will increase and their overall problem solving skills will improve. This same type of activity can be used in tantrum areas. For example, if your child routinely has a break down at a certain time or place, try acting out what the appropriate behavior would be in that occurrence.

***What would you do if . . .***

You get lost at the grocery store/mall

You are riding the metro/bus/public transit and become separated from your parents

You get left behind in the elevator at the mall

Someone walks into the bathroom stall that you are using

***Every day twenty-three hundred children are reported missing in the United States. Through the work of dedicated people and technology resources as many as 90 percent of these children can be recovered.***

***— FBI National Crime Information Center***

***What would you do if . . .***

You are at a restaurant and you have to wait a long time for your food

You are at a restaurant and they bring you food you don't like

You are grocery shopping and your mom and dad wouldn't let you have the treat you want

You find a toy you really want at the toy store and Mom says, "Not today."

**Mom:** "Tiff, we are on our way to the toy store to buy your brother a present. We are *only* buying something today for Adam because it is his birthday. I know you will see things there that you want, but we are only buying for Adam today. So let's practice some appropriate behavior before we get there."

**Tiffany:** "Okay, Mom."

**Mom:** "What will you do if you are at the store today and you see a toy that you want?"

**Tiffany:** "I will say, 'Look, Mom, just what I have been wanting.'"

**Mom:** "Oh, that is pretty honey, but remember what we talked about."

**Tiffany:** "Yes, Mom, I'm just showing you. We are shopping for Adam."

**Mom:** "Thank you, honey. Thanks for cooperating."

*Tiffany, age six*

***What would you do if . . .***

Someone on the street asks you for money

Someone on the street asks you for food

Someone you don't know asks you your name

Someone you don't know offers you candy/treat

***What would you do if . . .***

Mom or Dad is in the shower and someone rings the doorbell

You answer the phone and someone says "bad words"

Someone tells you a secret and says not to tell mom or dad

You answer the phone and the person on the phone wants to know your name

***What would you do if . . .***

You find a piece of candy on the floor (in the mall/parking lot, etc.)

You find some money or
a wallet

You see someone steal
something

You accidentally walk out of a
store with something in your
hand that does not belong to you

**Dad:** "What would you do if we are at the mall and you find a piece of candy on the floor?"

**William:** "I would pick it up and put it in my mouth!"

*William, age two*

## Kim's "What If" Payoff

Early one morning my sister and I took our kids to the park. After getting everyone settled, I ran to the car to get a diaper for the baby, while my sister said she would keep an eye on the kids. When I returned, I could see my daughter and her cousin entering the public restroom. Although we were the only people in the park, I was still uncomfortable with her using the restroom without adult supervision.

Due to a current news report concerning a child who had been attacked in a public restroom, we had recently had a "What Would You Do If" discussion about this very topic. I began to walk toward the restroom when I saw my daughter stop, say something to her cousin and run out of the restroom and back to where I stood. As she approached me she said, "Sorry, Mom, I started to walk in there with Becky, but then I remembered what we talked about. Bad things could happen in there and I need to have you or Aunt Heidi with me."

I praised her for remembering what we had talked about. Suddenly out of the corner of my eye I saw a man sitting alone on a table, near the side entrance to the restroom. While I have no idea if he truly posed a threat or not, I was haunted by the thoughts of what *could have* happened had the girls entered the restroom alone.

The few moments it took to prepare my daughter for this situation may have provided us with more of a payoff than we may ever know.

On the way home, Madie piped up from the backseat, "Mom, lets play 'What Would You Do If. . .'" I smiled to myself as we began another "What Would You Do If" journey.

Life is an adventure filled with twisting paths, marked by melodic streams on one side and plunging cliffs on the other. To those fortunate enough to walk that path hand in hand with a child we say; hold on tight, enjoy the ride *and* ask the right questions.